Beginner-Friendly Quilting

by Linda Causee

LEISURE ARTS, INC.
Maumelle, Arkansas

Produced by

Production Team

Creative Directors:	Jean Leinhauser and Rita Weiss
Book Design:	Linda Causee
Technical Editor:	Ann Harnden

Diagrams © 2016 by The Creative Partners LLC
Reproduced by special permission

We have made every effort to ensure that these instructions are accurate and complete. We cannot, however, be responsible for human error, typographical mistakes or variations in individual work.

Published by Leisure Arts, Inc.

© 2016 by Leisure Arts, Inc.

104 Champs Boulevard, STE. 100

Maumelle, AR 72113

www. leisurearts.com

Library of Congress Control Number: 2016942644

ISBN: 978-1-4647-5231-5

Introduction

You've just learned to quilt—or you learned how a long time ago and have now forgotten most of what you were taught. You think you know how to quilt because you've learned all of the necessary basics (whether someone taught you, you took a class, or perhaps you taught yourself online).

So now you are ready to make a quilt.

But, here comes the hard part. You may feel you know all the basics, and you are sure you can cut and sew the perfect pattern you'll surely find. But all of the patterns you find online, in pattern books or magazines seem too difficult. As for most of the easy ones, they don't look very attractive.

Well guess what? You've come to the right place. This is the book for you, the answer to all of your problems.

In this book, I've collected some of my favorite patterns that I used in my early quilting days: patterns for quilts that I enjoyed making, enjoyed using and was happy to give as gifts.

But—most important—all of the quilt patterns are intended for beginners just like you!

Now if you can't remember exactly what you learned (or maybe were never taught), spend some time with our General Directions on pages 56 to 61. Here, I've given you an explanation of how to work all of the instructions I've used in these patterns.

So get started making that first quilt. You'll not only be glad you did, but you'll be tempted to start making quilts for all your friends and relatives.

Linda Causee

Contents

Irish Chain

Approximate Size: 40" x 60"

You don't have to be Irish to want to make this quilt. It's one that's been a favorite of quilters for over 100 years, and it's sure to make you proud to wear the green!

Materials

½ yd dk green print

½ yd med green print

2 ¼ yds lt green print

1 yd floral print

1 ¾ yds backing

batting

Patterns

(pages 63, 64)

A Triangle

B Square

E Rectangle

K Square

Cutting

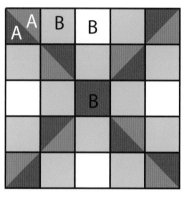

Block A (10" x 10" finished)

(make 8)

64 A Triangles, dk green print

8 B Squares, dk green print

64 A Triangles, med green print

96 B Squares, lt green print

32 B Squares, floral print

Block B (10" x 10" finished)

(Make 7)

28 B Squares, lt green print

28 E Rectangles, floral print

7 K Squares, floral print

Finishing

6 strips, 5 ½"-wide, lt green print (border)

6 strips, 2 ½"-wide, med green print (binding)

continued on page 8

Instructions

Making Block A

1. Sew a dk green A Triangle to a med green A Triangle; press seams to one side. Make a total of 8 patches.

2. For rows 1 and 5, sew two patches, 2 lt green B Squares, and a floral B Square together; press seams to one side.

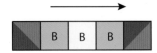

3. For rows 2 and 4, sew three lt green B Squares and two patches together; press seams in opposite direction.

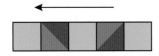

4. For row 3, sew two floral B Squares, two lt green B Squares and one dk green B Square together; press seams in opposite direction.

5. Sew rows together to complete Block A. Note that rows 4 and 5 are turned before sewing. Make a total of 8 Block A.

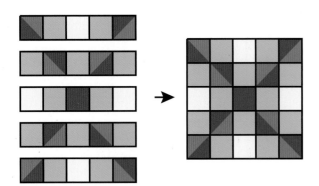

Making Block B

1. For rows 1 and 3, sew a lt green B Square to each end of a floral E Rectangle; repeat.

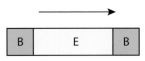

2. For row 2, sew a floral E Rectangle to opposite sides of a floral K Square.

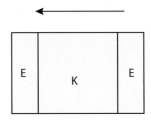

3. Sew rows 1, 2 and 3 together to complete Block B. Make a total of 7 Block B.

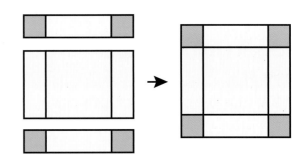

Finishing Your Quilt

1. Referring to the layout, place blocks in five rows of three blocks, alternating Blocks A and B.

2. Sew the blocks together in rows; press seams in opposite directions for rows. Sew rows together.

3. Refer to Adding Borders, page 58, to add border.

4. Refer to Finishing Your Quilt, pages 58 to 61, to complete your quilt.

Layout

9

Christmas Log Cabin

Approximate Size 52" x 62"

*The Log Cabin pattern has been a favorite among quilters for a long time.
Now just follow this pattern to turn it into a wonderful addition to your home when
it is time to celebrate Christmas. Make another version in every-day colors as well.*

Materials

¾ yd green print

⅝ yd beige print 1

¾ yd beige print 2

⅝ yd red print 1

2 ¾ yds red print 2

3 ¼ yds backing

batting

Patterns

(pages 62-64)

B Square

D Rectangle

E Rectangle

F Rectangle

G Rectangle

Cutting

Log Cabin Block (10" x 10" finished)
(make 20)

20 B Squares, green print

20 B Squares, beige print 1

20 D Rectangles each, beige print 1 and red print 1

20 E Rectangles each, beige print 2 and red print 1

20 F Rectangles each, beige print 2 and red print 2

20 G Rectangles, red print 2

Finishing

6 strips, 2 ½" -wide, green print (first border)

8 strips, 4 ½"-wide, red print 2 (second border)

9 strips, 2 ½"-wide, red print 2 (binding)

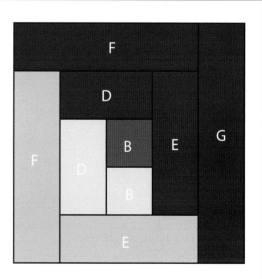

continued on page 12

Instructions

Making the Block

1. Sew a beige print 1 B Square to green print B Square; press seam toward beige print 1.

2. Sew a beige print 1 D Rectangle to the pair of squares. **Note:** *Be sure that the beige print 1 square is at the top when you sew.* Press seam toward beige print 1.

3. Turn the unit just made counterclockwise and sew a red print 1 D Rectangle; press seam toward strip just added.

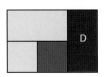

4. Turn the unit counterclockwise and sew a red print 1 E Rectangle; press seam toward strip just added.

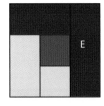

5. Turn the unit counterclockwise and sew a beige print 2 E Rectangle; press seam toward strip just added.

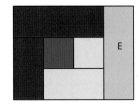

6. Turn the unit counterclockwise and sew a beige print 2 F Rectangle; press seam toward strip just added.

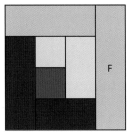

7. Turn the unit counterclockwise and sew a red print 2 F Rectangle; press seam toward strip just added.

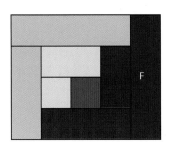

8. Turn the unit counterclockwise and sew a red print 2 G Rectangle; press seam toward strip just added. Make a total of 20 blocks.

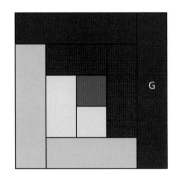

Finishing Your Quilt

1. Referring to the layout, place blocks in five rows of four blocks. Sew blocks together in rows; press seams in opposite directions for rows.

2. Sew rows together.

3. Refer to Adding Borders, page 58, to add first and second borders.

4. Refer to Finishing Your Quilt, pages 58 to 61, to complete your quilt.

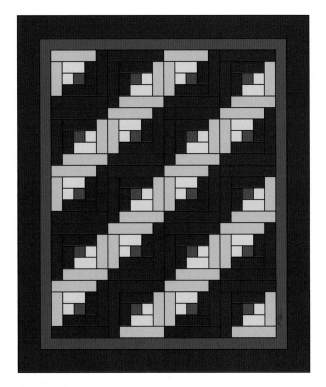

Layout

Whirling Pinwheels

Approximate Size 41" x 41"

An unusual design of pulsating pinwheels gives this little quilt a special charm. It certainly will be a conversation piece that will turn heads wherever it is displayed.

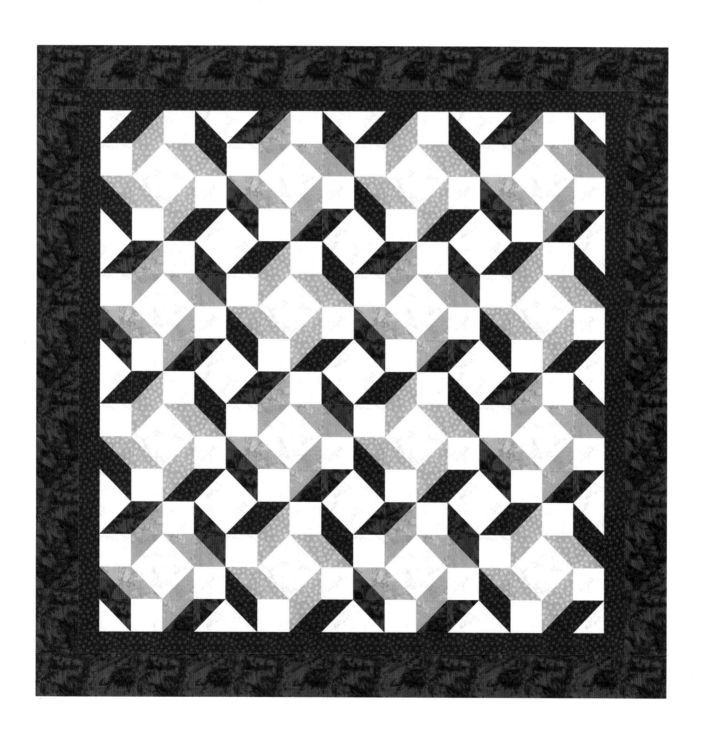

13

continued on page 14

Materials

¾ yd red print

⅓ yd pink print

1 ¼ yds dk green print

⅓ yd lt green print

1 yd off-white print

1 ¼ yds backing

batting

Patterns

(pages 63, 64)

A Triangle

B Square

Cutting

Whirling Pinwheel Block (8" x 8" finished)

(make 8, each color way)

64 A Triangles each, dk green print (red print)

64 A Triangles each, lt green print (pink print)

128 A Triangles, off-white print

64 B Squares, off-white print

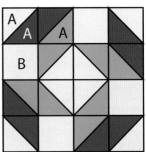

Finishing

2 strips, 2" x 32 ½", red print (first border-sides)

2 strips, 2" x 35 ½", red print (first border-top and bottom)

2 strips, 3 ½" x 35 ½", dk green print (second border-sides)

2 strips, 3 ½" x 41 ½", dk green print (second border - top and bottom)

6 strips, 2 ½"-wide, dk green print (binding)

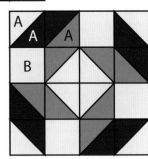

Instructions

Making the Blocks

1. Sew a dk green A Triangle to an off-white A Triangle; press seam toward dk green. Make four patch 1.

2. Sew a dk green A Triangle to a lt green A Triangle; press seam toward dk green. Make four patch 2.

3. Sew a lt green A Triangle to an off-white A Triangle; press seam toward lt green. Make four patch 3.

4. Sew a patch 1 to a patch 2; press seam to one side. Repeat 3 more times.

5. Sew an off-white B Square to a patch 3; press seam to opposite side. Repeat 3 more times.

6. Sew patches from steps 4 and 5 together; press seam to one side. Repeat 3 more times.

7. Sew two sections from step 6 together; press seam to one side. Repeat.

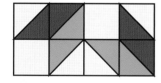

8. Sew sections from step 7 to complete block; press seam to one side. Make 8.

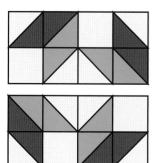 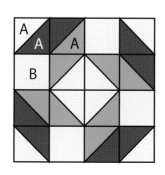

9. Sew a red A Triangle to an off-white A Triangle; press seam toward red. Make four patch 1.

10. Sew a red A Triangle to a pink A Triangle; press seam toward red. Make four patch 2.

11. Sew a pink A Triangle to an off-white A Triangle; press seam toward pink. Make four patch 3.

12. Sew a patch 1 to a patch 2; press seam to one side. Repeat 3 more times.

13. Sew an off-white B Square to a patch 3; press seam to opposite side. Repeat 3 more times.

14. Sew patches from steps 12 and 13 together; press seam to one side. Repeat 3 more times.

15. Sew two sections from step 14 together; press seam to one side. Repeat.

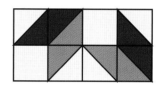

16. Sew sections from step 15 to complete block; press seam to one side. Make 8.

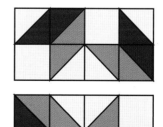 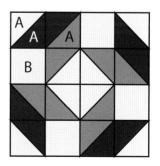

15

continued on page 16

Finishing Your Quilt

1. Referring to the layout, place blocks in four rows of four blocks, alternating red and green blocks.

2. Sew blocks together in rows; press seams for rows in opposite directions. Sew rows together.

3. Refer to Adding Borders, page 58, to add first and second borders to quilt.

4. Refer to Finishing your Quilt, pages 58 to 61, to complete your quilt.

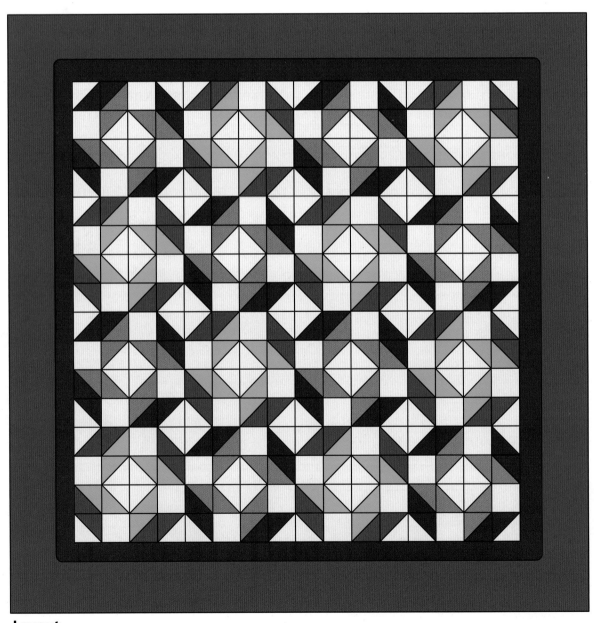

Layout

Diamonds

Approximate Size 60" x 60"

Diamonds are forever, and so will this lovely quilt become as it can be used to commemorate a special occasion for a special friend or relative.

17

continued on page 18

Materials

2 yds dk purple print

1 ½ yds lt purple print

⅞ yd lt cream print

⅞ yd med cream print

3 yds backing

batting

Patterns

(page 62)

L Triangle

Cutting

Diamond Block (12 " x 12" finished)

(make 16)

160 L Triangles, dk purple print

96 L Triangles, lt purple print

128 L Triangles, lt cream print

128 L Triangles, med cream print

Finishing

6 strips, 2 ½"-wide, lt purple print (first border)

7 strips, 4 ½"-wide, dk purple print (second border)

7 strips, 2 ½"-wide, dk purple print (binding)

Instructions

Making the Block

1. Sew a dk purple L Triangle to a med cream L Triangle; press seam toward dk purple. Make 4 patch 1.

2. Sew a dk purple L Triangle to a lt cream L Triangle; press seam toward dk purple. Make 6 patch 2.

3. Sew a lt purple L Triangle to a lt cream L Triangle; press seam toward lt purple. Make 2 patch 3.

4. Sew a lt purple L Triangle to a med cream L Triangle; press seam toward lt purple. Make 4 patch 4.

5. Sew a patch 1 to a patch 2; press seam to one side. Repeat.

6. Sew a patch 2 to a patch 3; press seam to opposite side. Repeat.

7. Sew units from steps 5 and 6 together; press seam to one side. Repeat.

8. Sew a patch 4 to a patch 2; press seams to one side. Repeat.

9. Sew a patch 1 to a patch 4; press seams to opposite side. Repeat.

10. Sew units from steps 8 and 9 together; press seam to one side. Repeat.

11. Sew units from steps 7 and 10 together; press seam to one side. Repeat.

12. Sew the units from step 11 together to complete block. Make 16 blocks.

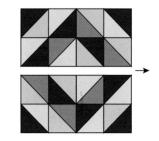 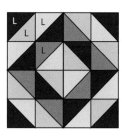

Finishing Your Quilt

1. Referring to the layout, place blocks in four rows of four blocks.

2. Sew blocks together in rows; press seams for rows in opposite directions. Sew rows together.

3. Refer to Adding Borders, page 58, to sew first and second borders to quilt top.

4. Refer to Finishing Your Quilt, pages 58 to 61, to complete your quilt.

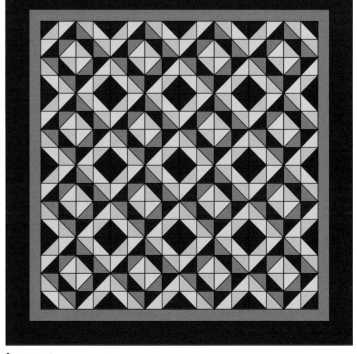

Layout

Diamond Path

Approximate Size 64" x 88"

What could be lovelier than a quilt that points to mysterious paths that run around and around the warmth of a lovely quilt.

Materials

2 ½ yds dk blue print

1 ¼ yds med blue print

1 ¼ yds lt blue print

3 yds turquoise print

5 yds backing

batting

Patterns

(pages 62, 64)

H Square

L Triangle

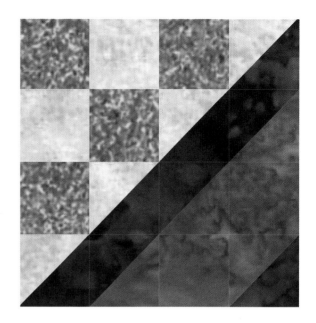

Cutting

Path Block (12" x 12" finished)

(make 24)

192 L Triangles, dk blue print

96 L Triangles, med blue print

48 H Squares, med blue print

96 L Triangles, lt blue print

48 H Squares, lt blue print

96 H Squares, turquoise print

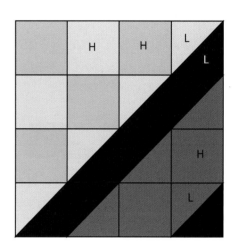

Finishing

7 strips, 3 ½"- wide, dk blue print (first border)

8 strips, 5 ½"-wide, turquoise print (second border)

9 strips, 2 ½"-wide, turquoise print (binding)

continued on page 22

Instructions

Making the Block

1. Sew a lt blue L Triangle to a dk blue L Triangle; press seam toward dk blue. Repeat for 3 more patch 1.

2. Sew a dk blue L Triangle to a med blue L Triangle; press seam toward dk blue. Repeat for 3 more patch 2.

3. For row 1, sew two turquoise H Squares, a lt blue H Square and a patch 1. Press seams to one side.

4. For row 2, sew a lt blue H Square, turquoise H Square, patch 1 and patch 2. Press seam to opposite side.

5. For row 3, sew a turquoise H Square, patch 1, patch 2 and med blue H Square. Press seam to one side.

6. For row 4, sew a patch 1, patch 2, med blue H Square and another patch 2. Press seams to opposite side.

7. Sew rows 1 and 2 together; sew rows 3 and 4 together. Then sew halves together to complete block. Press seams. Make 24 blocks.

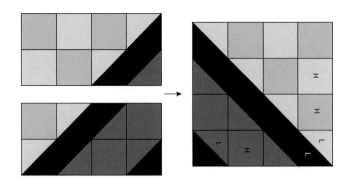

Finishing Your Quilt

1. Referring to the layout, place blocks in six rows of four blocks. Sew blocks in rows; press seams for rows in opposite directions. Sew rows together.

2. Refer to Adding Borders, page 58, to sew first and second borders to quilt top.

3. Refer to Finishing Your Quilt, pages 58 to 61, to complete your quilt.

Layout

22

Triple Hearts

Approximate Size 53 ½" x 53 ½"

Want to make a gift for a cherished mother, an adored grandmother, a perfect aunt or any other special lady in your life, then make this quilt decorated with hidden hearts and warm memories.

23

continued on page 24

Materials

¾ yd lt pink print

1 ⅝ yds med pink print

¼ yd red print

¾ yd white print

1 yd dk blue print

2 ½ yds backing

batting

Patterns

(pages 63, 64)

B Square

A Triangle

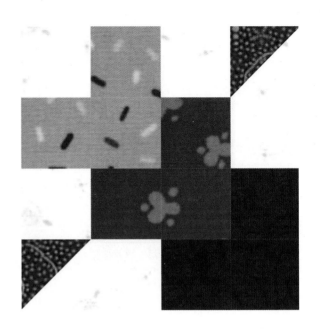

Cutting

Heart Block (8" x 8" finished)

(make 16)

48 B Squares each, lt pink, med pink and red prints

80 B Squares, white print

32 A Triangles, white print

32 A Triangles, dk blue print

Finishing

8 strips, 2" x 8 ½", dk blue print (sashing)

6 strips, 2" x 17 ½", dk blue print (sashing)

2 strips, 2 " x 36 ½", dk blue print (first border-sides)

2 strips, 2" x 39 ½", dk blue print (first border-top and bottom)

5 strips, 3 ½" -wide, lt pink print (second border)

6 strips, 4 ½"-wide, med pink print (third border)

6 strips, 2 ½"-wide, med pink print (binding)

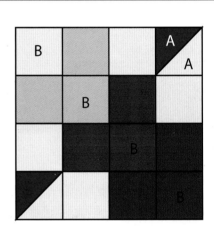

Instructions

Making the Block

1. Sew a dk blue A Triangle to a white print A Triangle; press seam toward dk blue.

2. For row 1, sew a white B Square, lt pink B Square, another white B Square and a triangle patch; press seam in one direction.

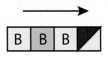

3. For row 2, sew two lt pink B Squares, a med pink B Square and white B Square; press seam in opposite direction.

4. For row 3, sew a white B Square, two med pink B Squares and a red B Square; press seams in one direction.

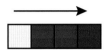

5. For row 4, sew a triangle patch, white B Square, and two red B Squares; press seams in opposite direction.

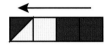

6. Sew rows 1 and 2 together; sew rows 3 and 4 together. Sew halves together to complete block. Make 16 blocks.

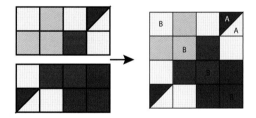

Finishing Your Quilt

1. Sew two Heart blocks together with a 2" x 8 ½" dk blue sashing strip in between. Repeat.

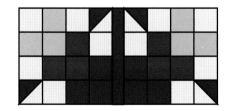

2. Sew the sections made in step one with a 2" x 17 ½" dk blue sashing strip between. Repeat for 3 more sections.

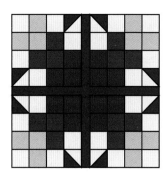

3. Sew two sections from step 2 together with a 2" x 17 ½" dk blue sashing strip in between. Repeat.

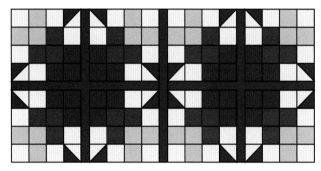

4. Sew sections from step 3 together with 2" x 36 ½" dk blue sashing strip in between.

5. Refer to Adding Borders, page 58, to sew the first and second borders to quilt top.

6. Refer to Finishing Your Quilt, pages 58 to 61, to complete your quilt.

Southwest Zigzag

Approximate Size 42" x 50"

The colors of a dramatic sunset over a southwestern desert are reflected in the fabrics making up this quilt while the striking zigzag pattern is reminiscent of design themes used in Native American lore.

Materials

1 ¼ yds turquoise print

1 yd lavender print

⅝ yd rust print

1 ¼ yds gold print

1 ½ yds backing

batting

Patterns

(pages 63, 64)

A Triangle

B Square

Cutting

Zigzag Block (8" x 8" finished)

(make 20)

160 A Triangles, turquoise print

80 B Squares, turquoise print

240 A Triangles, lavender print

40 A Triangles, rust print

40 A Triangles, gold print

Finishing

4 strips, 2 ½"-wide, rust print (first border)

5 strips, 3 ½" -wide, gold print (second border)

5 strips, 2 ½"-wide, gold print (binding)

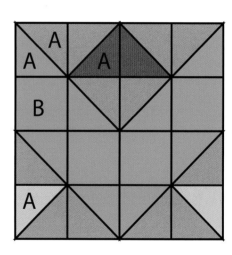

continued on page 28

Instructions

Making the Block

1. Sew a turquoise A Triangle to a lavender A Triangle; press seam toward one side. Make 8 patch 1.

2. Sew a lavender A Triangle to a rust A Triangle; press seam toward one side. Make two patch 2.

3. Sew a lavender A Triangle to a gold A Triangle; press seam toward one side. Make two patch 3.

4. For row 1, sew a patch 1, two patch 2, and another patch 1; press seams to one side.

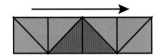

5. For row 2, sew a turquoise B Square, two patch 1 and another turquoise B Square; press seams in opposite direction.

6. For row 3, sew a patch 1, two turquoise B Squares, and another patch 1; press seams to one side.

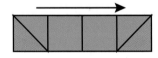

7. For row 4, sew a patch 3, two patch 1, and another patch 3; press seam in opposite direction.

8. Sew rows 1 and 2 together; press seam to one side. Sew rows 3 and 4 together; press seam to one side. Sew halves together to complete block. Make 20 blocks.

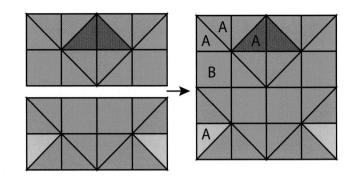

Finishing Your Quilt

1. Referring to the layout, place blocks in five rows of four blocks. Sew blocks in rows; press seams for rows in opposite directions. Sew rows together.

2. Refer to Adding Borders, page 58, to sew the first and second borders to the quilt top.

3. Refer to Finishing Your Quilt, pages 58 to 61, to complete your quilt.

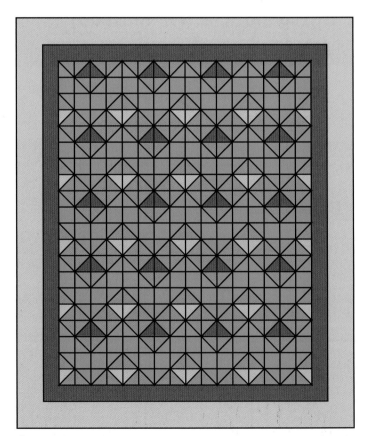

Layout

Summer Kaleidoscope

Approximate Size 46" x 54"

*Here's a quilt that you'll want to hang on the wall as if it were
a fine modern painting. Because the entire quilt is made only of triangles of
various colors, it will be so quick and easy to do that you'll be able to finish
it in record time and enjoy it for a lifetime.*

29

continued on page 30

Materials

¾ yd lt blue print

1 ½ yds dk blue print

½ yd orange print

¾ yd pink print

1 ⅛ yds green print

3 yds backing

batting

Patterns

(page 63)

A Triangle

Cutting

Pinwheel Block (8" x 8" finished)

(make 20)

160 A Triangles, lt blue print

80 A Triangles, dk blue print

80 A Triangles, orange print

160 A Triangles, pink print

160 A Triangles, green print

Finishing

4 strips, 3 ½"- wide, green print (first border)

5 strips, 4 ½"-wide, dk blue print (second border)

5 strips, 2 ½"-wide, dk blue print (binding)

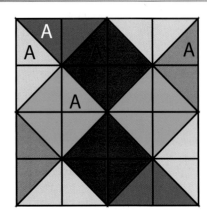

Instructions

Making the Block

1. Sew a lt blue A Triangle to a dk blue A Triangle; press seam to one side. Make 2 patch 1.

2. Sew a dk blue A Triangle to a pink A Triangle; press seam to one side. Make 2 patch 2.

3. Sew a lt blue A Triangle to a pink A Triangle; press seam to one side. Make 2 patch 3.

4. Sew a lt blue A Triangle to an orange A Triangle; press seam to one side. Make 2 patch 4.

5. Sew a lt blue A Triangle to a green A Triangle; press seam to one side. Make 2 patch 5.

6. Sew a green A Triangle to a pink A Triangle; press seam to one side. Make 4 patch 6.

7. Sew a green A Triangle to an orange A Triangle; press seam to one side. Make 2 patch 7.

8. Sew a patch 1 to a patch 2; press seam to one side. Sew a patch 5 to a patch 6; press seam to opposite side. Sew pairs together for four-patch 1. Repeat.

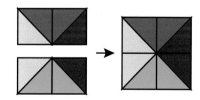

9. Sew a patch 3 to a patch 4; press seam to one side. Sew a patch 6 to a patch 7; press seam to opposite side. Sew pairs together for four-patch 2. Repeat.

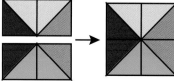

10. Sew a four-patch 1 and a four-patch 2 together; press seam to one side. Repeat.

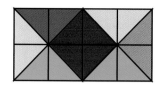

11. Sew units made in step 10 together to complete block. Make a total of 20 blocks.

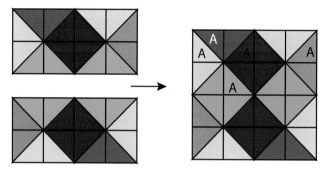

Finishing Your Quilt

1. Referring to the layout, place blocks in five rows of four blocks. Sew blocks together in rows; press seams for rows in opposite directions. Sew rows together.

2. Refer to Adding Borders, page 58, to add first and second borders to quilt top.

3. Refer to Finishing Your Quilt, pages 58 to 61, to complete your quilt.

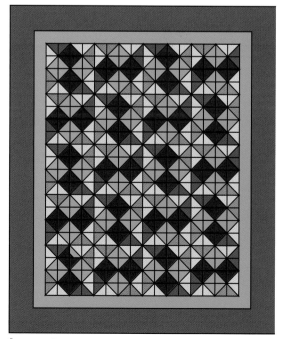

Layout

Crosses

Approximate Size 64" x 88"

Honor a special person with this quilt decorated with crosses that look as though they were carved from fine ivory. Who would believe that the quilt was made only with squares and triangles?

Materials

1 ⅝ yds purple print

1 ½ yds black print

2 ¾ yds dk red print

½ yd lt red print

5 yds backing

batting

Patterns

(pages 62, 64)

L Triangle

H Square

K Square

Cutting

Cross Block (12" x 12")

(make 24)

48 K Squares, purple print

48 H Squares, black print

48 L Triangles, dk red print

48 H Squares, dk red print

48 L Triangles, lt red print

48 H Squares, lt red print

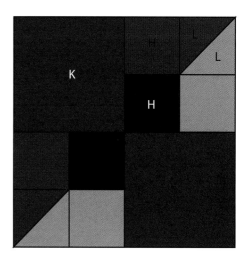

Finishing

7 strips, 3 ½"-wide, black print (first border)

8 strips, 5 ½"-wide, dk red print (second border)

8 strips, 2 ½"-wide, dk red print (binding)

continued on page 34

Instructions

Making the Block

1. Sew a lt red L Triangle to a dk red L Triangle; press seam to one side. Repeat.

2. Sew a dk red H Square to triangle patch made in step 1. Note position of triangle patch. Press seam toward dk red.

3. Sew a black H Square to a lt red H Square; press seam toward lt red.

4. Sew units from step 2 and 3 to make a four patch. Press seam to one side.

5. Sew a purple K Square to four patch; press seam toward purple Square.

6. Sew a triangle patch to a lt red H Square; press seam toward lt red H Square.

7. Sew a dk red H Square and a black H Square; press seam toward dk red H Square.

8. Sew units made in steps 6 and 7 to complete four patch; press seams to one side.

9. Sew four patch to purple K Square; press seam toward purple square.

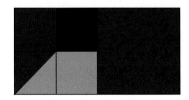

10. Sew units from steps 5 and 9 to complete block. Make 24 blocks.

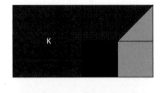 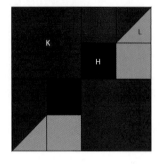

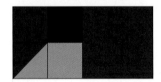

Finishing Your Quilt

1. Referring to the layout, place blocks in six rows of four blocks. Sew blocks together in rows; press seams for rows in opposite directions.

2. Refer to Adding Borders, page 58, to add first and second borders.

3. Refer to Finishing Your Quilt, pages 58 to 61, to complete your quilt.

Layout

Log Cabin Straight Furrows

Approximate Size 42" x 50"

The Log Cabin is one of the most recognizable and loved of all quilt patterns. This quilt uses the block named to honor the pioneers who worked the furrows on their plowed fields. As is true of all Log Cabin blocks, it is easy to do, and the results are always beautiful.

35

continued on page 36

Materials

1 ½ yds aqua print

¾ yd turquoise print

½ yd lt purple print

¾ yd dk purple print

2 ¼ yds backing

batting

Patterns

(page 63)

A Triangle

D, E, F Rectangles

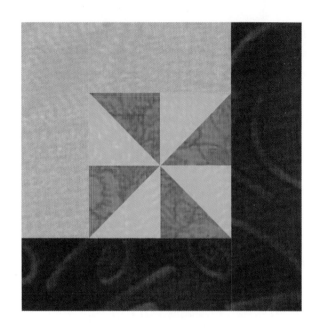

Cutting

Pinwheel Log Cabin Block (8" x 8" finished)

(make 20)

80 A Triangles, aqua print

80 A Triangles, turquoise print

20 D Rectangles, lt purple print

20 E Rectangles, lt purple print

20 E Rectangles, dk purple print

20 F Rectangles, dk purple print

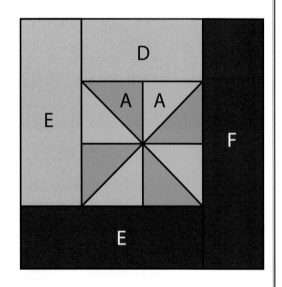

Finishing

5 strips, 2 ½"-wide, turquoise print (first border)

6 strips, 3 ½"-wide, aqua print (second border)

6 strips, 2 ½"-wide, aqua print (binding)

Instructions

Making the Block

1. Sew a turquoise A Triangle to an aqua A Triangle; press seam toward turquoise. Make four triangle squares.

2. Sew two triangle squares together; press seam to one side. Repeat.

3. Sew the units made in step 2 together to make pinwheel; press seam.

4. Sew a lt purple D Rectangle to one edge of pinwheel; press seam toward lt purple.

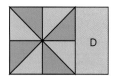

5. Turn pinwheel clockwise and sew lt purple E Rectangle; press seam toward lt purple.

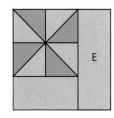

6. Turn pinwheel clockwise and sew dk purple E Rectangle; press seam toward dk purple.

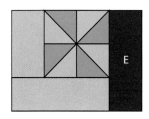

7. Turn pinwheel clockwise and sew dk purple F Rectangle to complete block; press seam toward dk purple. Make 20 blocks.

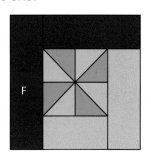

Finishing Your Quilt

1. Referring to the layout, place blocks in five rows of four blocks. Sew blocks together in rows; press seams for rows in opposite directions. Sew rows together.

2. Refer to Adding Borders, page 58, to sew first and second borders to quilt top.

3. Refer to Finishing Your Quilt, pages 58 to 61, to complete your quilt.

Layout

37

Vintage Redwork

Approximate Size 36" x 44"

Redwork quilts, popular during the late nineteenth and early twentieth centuries, were usually made with red embroidered blocks. This quick and easily pieced quilt celebrates that tradition with its blocks in red and white.

Materials

¾ yd cream/red print

1 ½ yds pink/red print

¾ yd bright red print

¾ yd dk red print

1 ¼ yds backing

batting

Pattern

(page 63)

A Triangle

Cutting

Vintage Block (8" x 8" finished)

(make 12)

192 A Triangles, cream/red print

96 A Triangles, pink/red print

48 A Triangles, bright red print

48 A Triangles, dk red print

Finishing

4 strips, 2 ½"-wide, bright red print (first border)

4 strips, 4 ½"-wide, pink/red print (second border)

5 strips, 2 ½"-wide, pink/red print (binding)

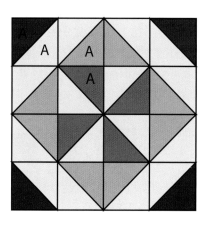

continued on page 40

Instructions

Making the Block

1. Sew dk red A Triangle to cream/red A Triangle; press seam toward dk red. Make 4 patch 1.

2. Sew cream/red A Triangle to pink/red A Triangle; press seam toward pink/red. Make 8 patch 2.

3. Sew a cream/red A Triangle to a bright red A Triangle; press seam toward bright red. Make 4 patch 3.

4. Sew a patch 1 to a patch 2; press seam to one side.

5. Sew a patch 2 to a patch 3; press seam in opposite direction.

6. Sew units from steps 4 and 5 together to make a four patch; press seam to one side. Repeat steps 4 and 5 for 3 more four patches.

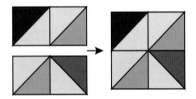

7. Sew two four patches together, noting position of blocks. Repeat.

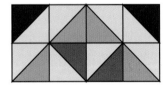

8. Sew halves together to complete block. Make 12 blocks.

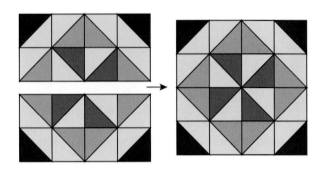

Finishing Your Quilt

1. Referring to the layout, place blocks in five rows of four blocks. Sew blocks together in rows; press seams for rows in opposite directions. Sew rows together.

2. Refer to Adding Borders, page 58, to sew first and second borders to quilt top.

3. Refer to Finishing Your Quilt, pages 58 to 61, to complete your quilt.

Layout

40

Sunny Stars

Approximate Size 74" x 86"

Bring the lovely night into the house. Since stars shine in a night sky, probably the only place you will see bright stars in a sunny sky is on a beautiful quilt like this.

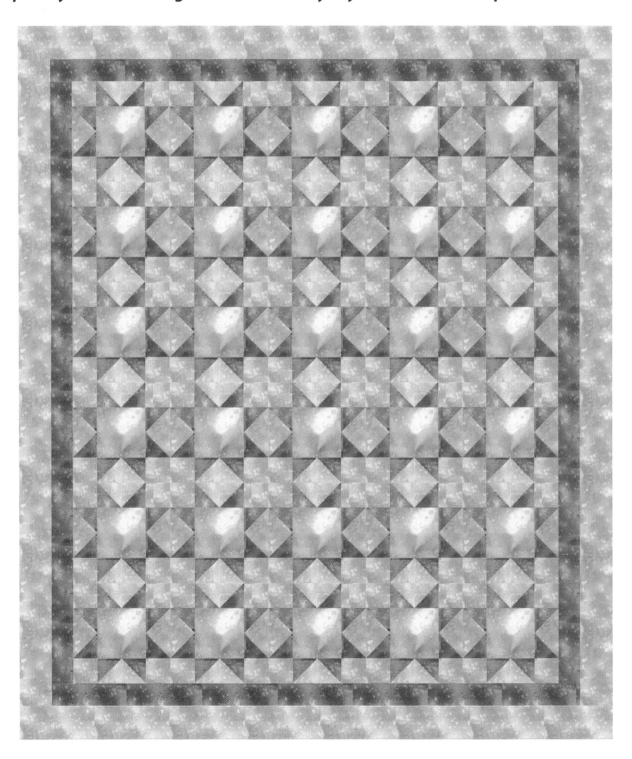

41

continued on page 42

Materials

3 ¾ yds blue print

1 yd lt orange print

2 yds dk orange print

5 yds backing

batting

Patterns

(pages 62, 64)

L Triangle

H Square

K Square

Cutting

Star Block (12" x 12" finished)

(make 30)

120 H Squares, blue print

240 L Triangles, blue print

30 K Squares, lt orange print

240 L Triangles, dk orange print

Finishing

8 strips, 3 ½"-wide, dk orange print (first border)

8 strips, 4 ½"-wide, blue print (second border)

9 strips, 2 ½"-wide, blue print (binding)

Instructions

Making the Block

1. Sew a dk orange L Triangle to a blue L Triangle; press seam to one side. Make 8 Triangle patches.

2. Sew two triangle patches together; press seam to one side. Repeat.

3. Sew units just made to opposite sides of lt orange K Square; press seams toward lt orange square.

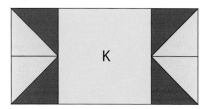

4. Sew two triangle patches together; press seam to one side. Repeat.

5. Sew a lt blue H Square to opposite ends of unit just made; press seam toward lt blue Square. Repeat.

6. Sew units just made to top and bottom of unit made in step 3 to complete block. Press seams to one side. Make a total of 30 blocks.

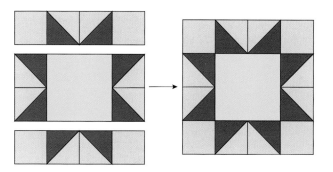

Finishing Your Quilt

1. Referring to the layout, place blocks in six rows of five blocks. Sew blocks together in rows; press seams for rows in opposite directions. Sew rows together.

2. Refer to Adding Borders, page 58, to add first and second borders to quilt top.

3. Refer to Finishing Your Quilt, pages 58 to 61, to complete your quilt.

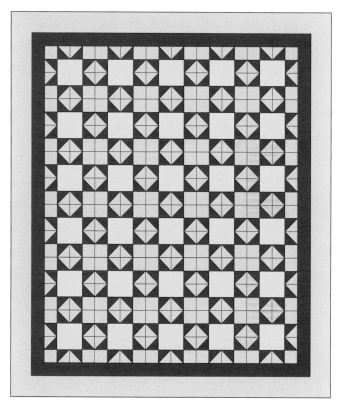

Layout

Quilt for a Man Cave

Approximate Size 72" x 84"

What man wouldn't appreciate a warm quilt like this for his special room?

Materials

3 yds gold print

1 ¼ yds med brown print

2 yds dk brown print

5 yds backing

batting

Patterns

(page 62)

C Triangle

M Triangle

Cutting

Zigzag Block (12" x 12" finished)

(make 30)

150 C Triangles, gold print

60 M Triangles, gold print

150 C Triangles, med brown print

60 M Triangles, med brown print

150 C Triangles, dk brown print

60 M Triangles, dk brown print

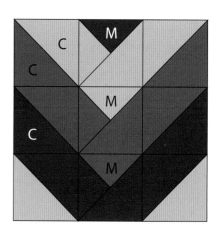

Finishing

9 strips, 2 ½"-wide, dk brown print (first border)

10 strips, 4 ½"-wide, gold print (second border)

10 strips, 2 ½"-wide, gold print (binding)

45

continued on page 46

Instructions

Making the Block

1. Sew a gold C Triangle to a med brown C Triangle; press seam toward med brown. Repeat for two patch 1.

2. Sew a gold M Triangle to a dk brown M Triangle; press seam toward dk brown. Sew to a gold C Triangle for patch 2.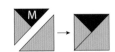

3. Sew a med brown C Triangle to a dk brown C Triangle; press seam toward dk brown. Repeat for two patch 3.

4. Sew a gold M Triangle to a med brown M Triangle; press seam toward med brown. Sew to med brown C Triangle for patch 4.

5. Sew a gold C Triangle to a dk brown C Triangle; press seam toward dk brown for patch 5. Repeat for two patch 5.

6. Sew a med brown M Triangle to a dk brown M Triangle; press seam toward dk brown. Sew to dk brown C Triangle for patch 6.

7. For row 1, sew a patch 1 to opposite sides of a patch 2. Press seams to one side.

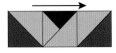

8. For row 2, sew a patch 3 to opposite sides of a patch 4. Press seams in opposite direction.

9. For row 3, sew a patch 5 to opposite sides of a patch 6. Press seams to one side.

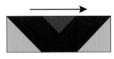

10. Sew rows together to complete block. Press seams to one side. Make a total of 30 blocks.

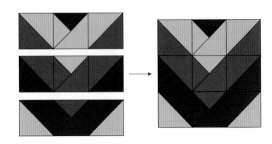

Finishing Your Quilt

1. Referring to the layout, place blocks in six rows of five blocks. Sew blocks together in rows; press seams for rows in opposite directions. Sew rows together.

2. Refer to Adding Borders, page 58, to sew first and second borders to quilt top.

3. Refer to Finishing Your Quilt, pages 58 to 61, to complete your quilt.

Layout

46

Pinwheel Plaid

Approximate Size 54" x 63"

Delightful pinwheels dance across this quilt creating an enchanting plaid pattern as they do.

47

continued on page 48

Materials

¾ yd lt peach print

¾ yd med peach print

⅞ yd dk peach print

3 ½ yds turquoise print

3 yds backing

batting

Patterns

(pages 62, 64)

H Square

L Triangle

Cutting

Nine Patch Block (9" x 9" finished)

(make 30)

120 L Triangles, lt peach print

120 H Squares, med peach print

30 H Squares, dk peach print

120 L Triangles, turquoise print

Finishing

6 strips, 2"-wide, dk peach print (first border)

6 strips, 3 ½"-wide, turquoise print (second border)

7 strips, 2 ½"-wide, turquoise print (binding)

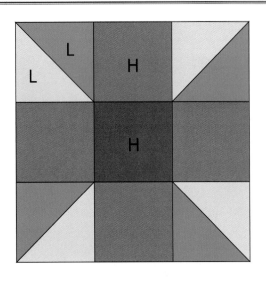

Instructions

Making the Block

1. Sew a lt peach L Triangle to a turquoise L Triangle; press seam toward turquoise. Make four triangle patches.

2. For rows 1 and 3, sew a triangle patch on opposite sides of a med peach H Square; press seams toward med peach. Repeat.

3. For row 2, sew a med peach H Square on opposite sides of a dk peach H Square; press seams toward med peach.

4. Sew rows together to complete block. Make 30 blocks.

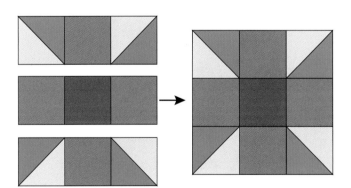

Finishing Your Quilt

1. Referring to the layout, place blocks in six rows of five blocks. Sew blocks together in rows; press seams for rows in opposite directions. Sew rows together.

2. Refer to Adding Borders, page 58, to add the first and second borders.

3. Refer to Finishing Your Quilt, pages 58 to 61, to complete your quilt.

Layout

Pinwheels Among the Stars

Approximate Size 58" x 70"

Lovely stars may serve as the main attraction in this quilt, but the yellow pinwheels sneak in to add additional charm.

Materials

1 yd lt yellow print

½ yd med yellow print

1 ¾ yds turquoise print

2 ½ yds blue print

3 ½ yds backing

batting

Patterns

(page 62)

L Triangle

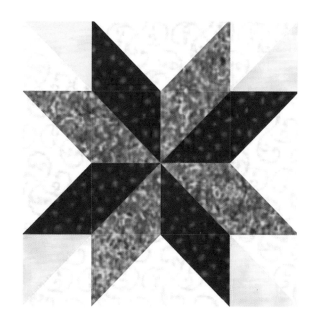

Cutting

Star Block (12" x 12" finished)

(make 12)

144 L Triangles, lt yellow print

48 L Triangles, med yellow print

96 L Triangles, turquoise print

96 L Triangles, blue print

Finishing

6 strips, 5 ½"-wide, turquoise print (first border)

6 strips, 6 ½"-wide, blue print (second border)

7 strips, 2 ½"-wide, blue print (binding)

continued on page 52

Instructions

Making the Block

1. Sew a lt yellow L Triangle to a med yellow L Triangle; press seam toward med yellow. Make four patch 1.

2. Sew a lt yellow L Triangle to a blue L Triangle; press seam toward blue. Make four patch 2.

3. Sew a yellow L Triangle to a turquoise L Triangle; press seam toward turquoise. Make four patch 3.

4. Sew a turquoise L Triangle to a blue L Triangle; press seam toward blue. Make four patch 4.

5. Sew a patch 1 to a patch 2; press seam to one side.

6. Sew a patch 3 to a patch 4; press seam in opposite direction.

7. Sew units from steps 5 and 6 together; press seam to one side.

8. Repeat steps 5, 6 and 7 for 3 more sections.

9. Sew two units together; press seams to one side. Repeat.

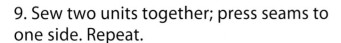

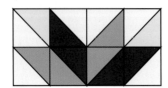

10. Sew halves together to complete block; press seam to one side. Make 12 blocks.

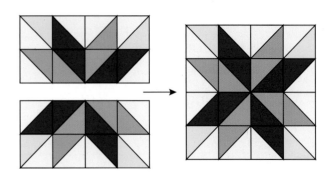

Finishing Your Quilt

1. Referring to the layout, place blocks in four rows of three blocks. Sew blocks together in rows; press seams for rows in opposite directions. Sew rows together.

2. Refer to Adding Borders, page 58, to sew first and second borders to quilt top.

3. Refer to Finishing Your Quilt, pages 58 to 61, to complete your quilt.

Layout

Basket Weave

Approximate Size 74" x 86"

Just add the bright colored rectangles together, and watch the quilt appear as if by magic.

53

continued on page 54

Materials

⅞ yd pink print

1 ¾ yds red print

⅞ yd burgundy print

⅞ yd lt green

⅞ yd med green

2 ½ yds dk green

5 yds backing

batting

Patterns

(page 63)

E Rectangle

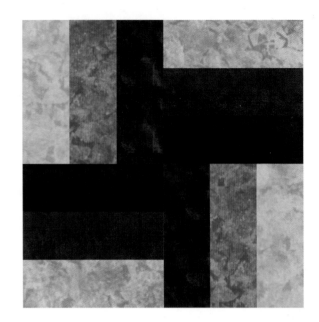

Cutting

Basket Weave Block (12" x 12" finished)

(make 30)

60 E Rectangles each, pink, red, burgundy, lt green, med green and dk green prints

Finishing

7 strips, 3 ½"-wide, red print (first border)

8 strips, 4 ½"-wide, dk green print (second border)

8 strips, 2 ½"-wide, dk green print (binding)

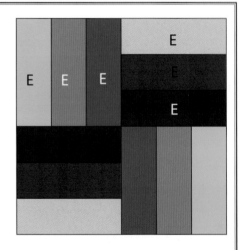

Instructions

Making the Block

1. Sew a lt green, med green and dk green E Rectangle together; press seams toward dk green. Repeat.

2. Sew a pink, red and burgundy E Rectangle together; press seams toward burgundy. Repeat.

3. Sew a green and red section together; press seam toward green. Repeat.

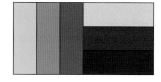

4. Sew halves together to complete block; press seam to one side. Make 30 blocks.

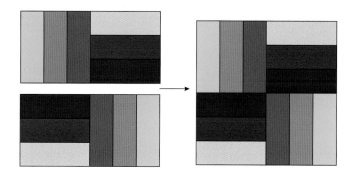

Finishing Your Quilt

1. Referring to the layout, place blocks in six rows of five blocks. Sew blocks together in rows; press seams for rows in opposite directions. Sew rows together.

2. Refer to Adding Borders, page 58, to sew first and second borders to quilt top.

3. Refer to Finishing Your Quilt, pages 58 to 61, to complete your quilt.

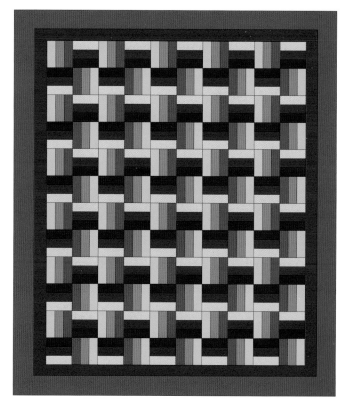

Layout

General Directions

Fabric

For over a hundred years, quilts have been made with 100% cotton fabric, the choice for most quilters.

There are many properties in cotton that make it especially well-suited to quilt making. There is less distortion in cotton fabric, thereby affording the quilter greater security in making certain that even the smallest bits of fabric will fit together. Because a quilt block made of cotton can be ironed flat with a steam iron, a puckered area, created by mistake, can be fixed. The sewing machine needle can move through cotton with a great deal of ease when compared to some synthetic fabrics. While you may find that quilt artists today often use other kinds of fabric, to create the quilts quickly and accurately, 100% cotton is strongly recommended.

Cotton fabric today is produced in so many wonderful and exciting combinations of prints and solids that it is often difficult to pick colors for your quilt. We've chosen our favorite colors for these quilts, but don't be afraid to make your own choices.

For years, quilters were advised to prewash all of their fabric to test for colorfastness and shrinkage. Now most quilters don't bother to prewash all of their fabric but they do pretest it. Cut a strip about 2" wide from each piece of fabric that you will use in your quilt. Measure both the length and the width of the strip. Then immerse it in a bowl of very hot water, using a separate bowl for each piece of fabric. Be especially concerned about reds and dark blues because they have a tendency to bleed if the initial dyeing was not done properly. If it's one of your favorite fabrics that's bleeding, you might be able to salvage the fabric. Try washing the fabric in very hot water until you've washed out all of the excess dye. Unfortunately, fabrics that continue to bleed after they have been washed repeatedly will bleed forever. So eliminate them right at the start.

Now, take each one of the strips and iron them dry with a hot iron. Be especially careful not to stretch the strip. When the strips are completely dry, measure and compare them to your original strip. If all of your fabric is shrinking the same amount, you don't have to worry about uneven shrinkage in your quilt. When you wash the final quilt, the puckering that will result may give you the look of an antique quilt. If you don't want this look, you are going to have to wash and dry all of your fabric before you start cutting. Iron the fabric using some spray starch or sizing to give fabric a crisp finish.

If you are never planning to wash your quilt, i.e. your quilt is intended to be a wall hanging such as many of the quilts in this collection, you could eliminate the pre-testing process. You may run the risk, however, of some future relative to whom you have willed your quilts deciding that the wall hanging needs freshening by washing.

Before beginning to work, make sure that your fabric is absolutely square. If it is not, you will have difficulty cutting square pieces. Fabric is woven with crosswise and lengthwise threads. Lengthwise threads should be parallel to the selvage (that's the finished edge along the sides; sometimes the fabric company prints its name along the selvage), and crosswise threads should be perpendicular to the selvage. If fabric is off grain, you can usually straighten it by pulling gently on the true bias in the opposite direction to the off-grain edge. Continue doing this until the crosswise threads are at a right angle to the lengthwise threads.

Templates

All of the templates used to make the quilts in this book are on pages 62 through 64. Photocopy the templates needed for your project then glue the templates onto plastic or heavy cardboard. When you are certain that your glue has dried, cut out your templates. If your templates become worn, simply repeat the process. If you are planning to do your piecing by machine, cut out your templates on the solid line. If you are piecing by hand, cut out your templates on the broken lines. The seam allowances for hand piecing will be added later when you cut out the pieces. It's always a good idea to write the template's letter in the center of the template.

Cutting

For Machine Piecing

Lay the template (with the ¼" seam allowance added) on the wrong side of the fabric near the top left edge of the material but not on the selvage; place it so that as many straight sides of the piece as possible are parallel to the crosswise and lengthwise grain of the fabric. Trace around the template with a marking tool such as a hard lead pencil. This will be your cutting line; use a sharp scissors or a rotary cutter and cut accurately.

The traditional seam allowance in quilting is ¼" so be certain that you sew each seam with a ¼" seam allowance. After you have joined two pieces together, press the seams flat to one side, not open.

For Hand Piecing

Lay the template, cut on the broken lines, on the fabric as described above for Machine Piecing. Trace around the template with your marking tool. **This will be your stitching line.**

Now measure ¼" around this shape. With a ruler, draw this second line which is your cutting line. The seam allowance does not have to be perfect since it will not show, but the stitching line must be perfectly straight or the pieces will not fit together.

Making a Quilt

Sewing the Blocks Together

Once all of the blocks for your quilt have been made, place them on a flat surface such as a design wall or floor to decide on the best placement.

Sew the blocks together. You can do this by sewing the blocks in rows, then sewing the rows together; or, sew the blocks in pairs then sew pairs together. Continue sewing in pairs until entire quilt top is sewn together.

Adding Borders

Borders are usually added to a quilt sides first, then top and bottom.

Step 1: Measure the quilt top lengthwise and cut two border strips to that length by the width measurement given in the project instructions. Strips may have to be pieced to achieve the correct length. To make the joining seam less noticeable, sew the strips together diagonally. Place two strips right sides together at right angles. Sew a diagonal seam. **(Diagram 1)**

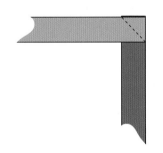

Step 2: Trim excess fabric ¼" from stitching. **(Diagram 2)**

Step 3: Press seam open. **(Diagram 3)**

Step 4: Sew strips to the sides of the quilt. Now measure the quilt top crosswise, being sure to include the borders you have just added. Cut two border strips, following the width measurement given in the instructions.

Step 5: Add these borders to the top and bottom of the quilt. Repeat this process for any additional borders. Use the ¼" seam allowance at all times and press all of the seams to the darker side. Press the quilt top carefully.

Finishing Your Quilt

Attaching the Batting and Backing

There are a number of different types of batting on the market today including the new fusible battings that eliminate the need for basting. Your choice of batting will depend upon how you are planning to use your quilt. If the quilt is to serve as a wall hanging, you will probably want to use a thin cotton batting. A quilt made with a thin cotton or cotton/polyester blend works best for machine quilting. Very thick polyester batting should be used only for tied quilts.

The best fabric for quilt backing is 100% cotton fabric. If your quilt is larger than the available fabric you will have to piece your backing fabric. When joining the fabric, try not to have a seam going down the center. Instead cut off the selvages and make a center strip that is about 36" wide and have narrower strips at the sides. Seam the pieces together and carefully iron the seams open. (This is one of the few times in making a quilt that a seam should be pressed open.) Several fabric manufacturers are now selling fabric in 90" or 108"-widths for use as backing fabric.

It is a good idea to remove the batting from its wrapping 24 hours before you plan to use it and open it out to full size. You will find that the batting will now lie flat when you are ready to use it.

The batting and the backing should be cut about one to two inches larger on all sides than the quilt top. Place the backing wrong side up on a flat surface. Smooth out the batting on top of this, matching the outer edges. Center the quilt top, right side up, on top of the batting.

Now the quilt layers must be held together before quilting, and there are several methods for doing this:

Safety-pin Basting: Starting from the center and working toward the edges, pin through all layers at one time with large safety pins. The pins should be placed no more than 4" apart. As you work, think of your quilting plan to make sure that the pins will avoid prospective quilting lines.

Thread Basting: Baste the three layers together with long stitches. Start in the center and sew toward the edges in a number of diagonal lines.

Quilt-gun Basting: This handy trigger tool pushes nylon tags through all layers of the quilt. Start in the center and work toward the outside edges. The tags should be placed about 4" apart. You can sew right over the tags, which can then be easily removed by cutting them off with scissors.

Spray or Heat-Set Basting: Several manufacturers have spray adhesives available especially for quilters. Apply these products by following the manufacturers' directions. You might want to test these products before you use them to make sure that they meet your requirements.

Fusible Iron-on Batting: These battings are a wonderful new way to hold quilt layers together without using any of the other time-consuming methods of basting. Again, you will want to test these battings to be certain that you are happy with the results. Follow the manufacturers' directions.

Quilting

If you like the process of hand quilting, you can–of course–finish these projects by hand quilting. However, if you want to finish these quilts quickly, you will want to use a sewing machine for quilting.

If you have never used a sewing machine for quilting, you may want to find a book and read about the technique. You do not need a special machine for quilting. Just make sure that your machine has been oiled and is in good working condition.

If you are going to do machine quilting, you should invest in an even-feed foot. This foot is designed to feed the top and bottom layers of a quilt evenly through the machine. The foot prevents puckers from forming as you machine quilt. Use a fine transparent nylon thread in the top and regular sewing thread in the bobbin.

Quilting in the ditch is one of the easiest ways to machine quilt.

This is a term used to describe stitching along the seam line between two pieces of fabric. Using your fingers, pull the blocks or pieces apart slightly and machine stitch right between the two pieces. The stitching will look better if you keep the stitching to the side of the seam that does not have the extra bulk of the seam allowance under it. The quilting will be hidden in the seam.

Free-form machine quilting can be used to quilt around a design or to quilt a motif. The quilting is done with a darning foot and the feed dogs down on the sewing machine. It takes practice to master Free-form quilting because you are controlling the movement of the quilt under the needle rather than the sewing machine moving the quilt. You can quilt in any direction—up and down, side-to-side and even in circles—without pivoting the quilt around the needle. Practice this quilting method before trying it on your quilt.

Attaching the Continuous Machine Binding

Once the quilt has been quilted, it must be bound to cover the raw edges.

Step 1: Start by trimming the backing and batting even with the quilt top. Measure the quilt top and cut enough 2 ½" wide strips to go around all four sides of the quilt plus 12". Join the strips end to end with diagonal seams and trim the corners. **(Diagram 4)**

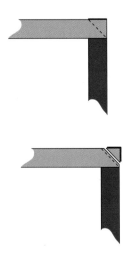

Press the seams open. **(Diagram 5)**

Step 2: Cut one end of the strip at a 45-degree angle and press under ¼". **(Diagram 6)**

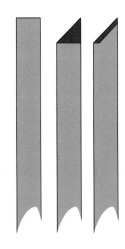

Step 3: Press entire strip in half lengthwise, wrong sides together. **(Diagram 7)**

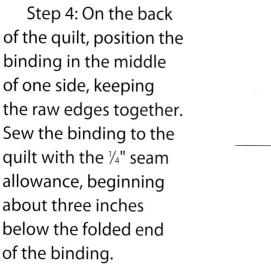

Step 4: On the back of the quilt, position the binding in the middle of one side, keeping the raw edges together. Sew the binding to the quilt with the $\frac{1}{4}$" seam allowance, beginning about three inches below the folded end of the binding.
(Diagram 8)

At the corner, stop $\frac{1}{4}$" from the edge of the quilt and backstitch.

Step 5: Fold binding away from quilt so it is at a right angle to edge just sewn. Then, fold the binding back on itself so the fold is on the quilt edge and the raw edges are aligned with the adjacent side of the quilt. Begin sewing at the quilt edge.
(Diagram 9)

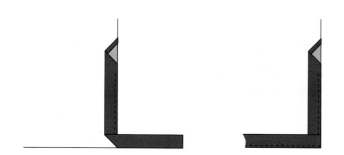

Step 6: Continue in the same way around the remaining sides of the quilt. Stop about 2" away from the starting point. Trim any excess binding and tuck it inside the folded end. Finish the stitching.
(Diagram 10)

Step 7: Fold the binding to the front of the quilt so the seam line is covered; machine-stitch the binding in place on the front of the quilt. Use a straight stitch or tiny zigzag with invisible or matching thread. If you have a sewing machine that does embroidery stitches, you may want to use your favorite stitch.

Labeling Your Quilt

Always sign and date your quilt when finished. You can make a label by cross-stitching or embroidering or even writing on a label with a permanent marking pen on the back of your quilt. If you are friends with your computer, you can even create an attractive label on the computer.

Template Patterns

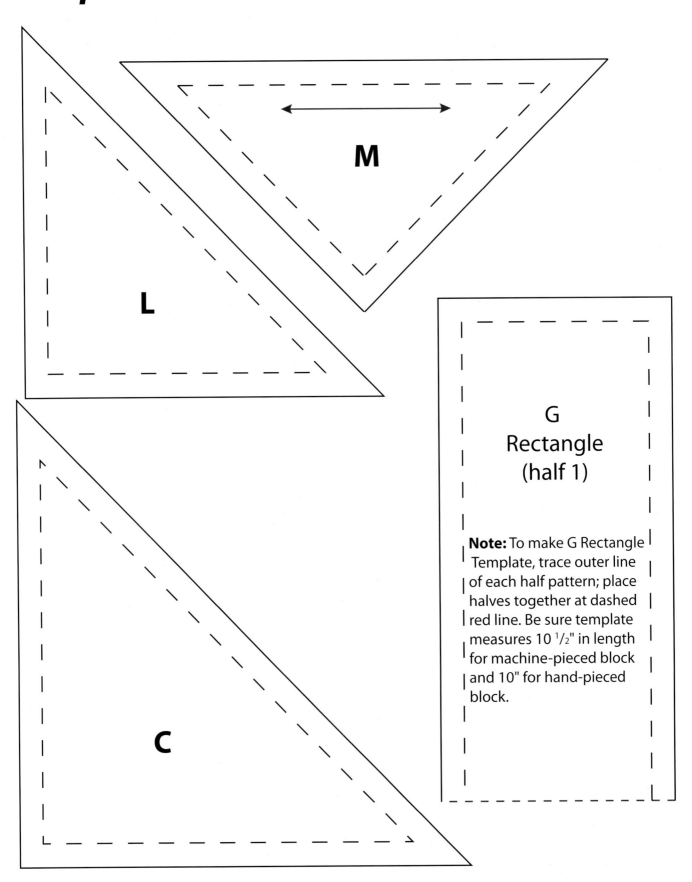

L

M

C

G
Rectangle
(half 1)

Note: To make G Rectangle Template, trace outer line of each half pattern; place halves together at dashed red line. Be sure template measures 10 $\frac{1}{2}$" in length for machine-pieced block and 10" for hand-pieced block.

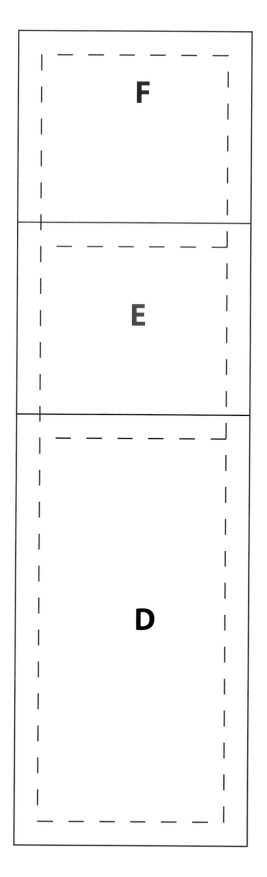

F

E

D

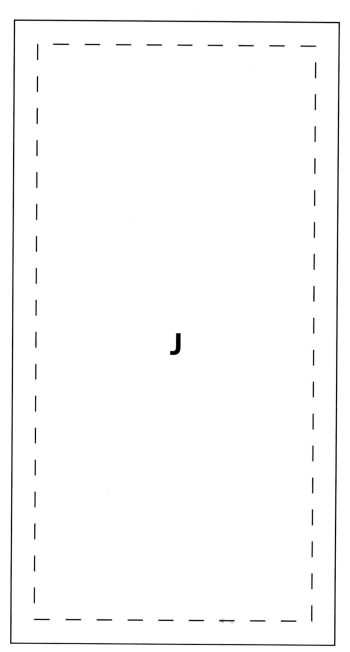

J

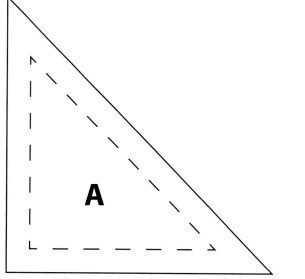

A

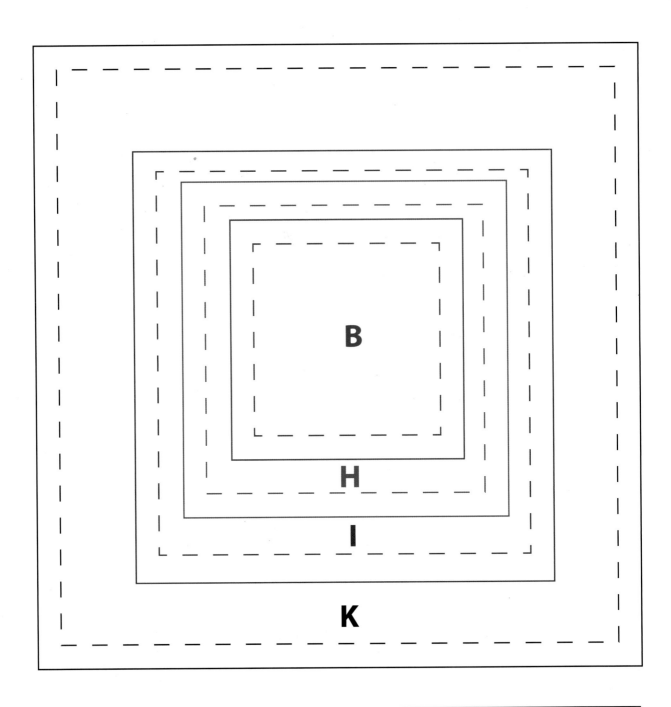

B

H

I

K

Note: To make G Rectangle Template, trace outer line of each half pattern; place halves together at dashed red line. Be sure template measures 10 ½" in length for machine-pieced block and 10" for hand-pieced block.

G
Rectangle
(half 2)